SECRET SEVEN WIN THROUGH

Secret Seven Win Through

Enid Blyton

Hodder
Children's
Books

a division of Hodder Headline plc

First published in Great Britain in 1955
by Hodder and Stoughton

Revised edition 1992

10 9

A Catalogue record for this book is available from the British Library

ISBN 0 340 56986 7

Photoset by Rowland Phototypesetting Ltd,
Bury St Edmunds, Suffolk

Printed and bound in Great Britain by
Clays Ltd, St Ives plc

Hodder Children's Books
a division of Hodder Headline plc
338 Euston Road
London NW1 3BH

Contents

1 The holidays begin

'Easter holidays at last!' said Peter. 'I thought they were never coming. Didn't you, Janet?'

'Yes. It was a dreadfully long term,' said Janet. 'We've broken up now though, thank goodness. Don't you love the first day of the hols, Peter?'

'You bet! I get a lovely *free* sort of feeling,' said Peter, 'and the hols seem to stretch out in front of me for ages and ages. Let's have some fun, Janet!'

'Yes, let's! April's a lovely month – it's warm, and sunny too, and Mummy will let us off on picnics any day we like,' said Janet. 'Scamper, do you hear that? Picnics, I said – and that means rabbit-hunting for you, and long, long walks.'

'Woof!' said Scamper at once, his tail thumping on the floor, and his eyes bright.

'You're the best and finest golden spaniel in the whole world!' said Janet, stroking his silky head. 'And I do so love your long, droopy ears, Scamper. You like it when we have holidays, don't you?'

'Woof!' said Scamper again, and thump-thump-thump went his tail.

'I vote we have a meeting of the Secret Seven as soon as we can,' said Peter. 'Tomorrow, if possible. Picnics and things are much more fun if we all go together.'

'Yes. Let's have a meeting,' said Janet. 'What with exams and one thing and another all the Secret Seven have forgotten about the Society. I haven't thought a word about it for at least three weeks. Gosh – what's the password?'

'Oh, Janet – you haven't forgotten that *surely*?' said Peter.

'You tell me,' said Janet, but Peter wouldn't. 'You don't know it yourself!' said Janet. 'I bet you don't!'

'Don't be silly,' said Peter. 'You'll have to remember it by tomorrow, if we have a meeting! Where's your badge? I expect you've lost that.'

'I have *not*,' said Janet. 'But I bet some of the others will have lost theirs. Somebody always does when we don't have a meeting for some time.'

'Better write out short notes to the other five,' said Peter. 'And tell them to come along tomorrow. Got some note-paper, Janet?'

'Yes, I have. But I don't feel a bit like sitting

down and writing the first day of the hols,' said Janet. 'You can jolly well help to write them.'

'No. I'll bike round to all the others and deliver the notes for you,' said Peter.

'Now it's *you* who are silly,' said Janet. 'If you're going to everyone's house, why not *tell* them about the meeting. All this note-writing! You just *tell* them.'

'All right. It just seems more *official* if we send out notes for a meeting, that's all,' said Peter. 'What time shall we have it?'

'Oh, half-past ten, I should think,' said Janet. 'And just warn Jack that he's not to let his horrid sister Susie know, or she'll come banging at the door, shouting out some silly password at the top of her voice.'

'Yes. I'll tell him,' said Peter. 'The worst of it is, Susie is so jolly sharp. She always seems to smell out anything to do with the Secret Seven.'

'She would be a better person to have *in* a club than out of it,' said Janet. 'But we'll never, never let her into ours.'

'Never,' said Peter. 'Anyway, we can't be more than seven, or we wouldn't be the Secret Seven.'

'Woof!' said Scamper.

'He says he belongs, even if we're seven and he makes the eighth!' said Janet. 'You're just a hanger-on, Scamper, but we simply couldn't do without you.'

'Well, I'm going to get my bike,' said Peter, getting up. 'I'll go round and tell all the others. See you later, Janet. Coming, Scamper?'

Off he went, and was soon cycling to one house after another. He went to Colin first, who was delighted to hear the news.

'Good!' he said. 'Half-past ten? Right, I'll be there. I say – whatever's the password, Peter?'

'You've got all day to think of it!' said Peter, with a grin, and rode off to Jack's. Jack was in the garden, mending a puncture in the back wheel of his bicycle. He was very pleased to see Peter.

'Meeting of the Secret Seven tomorrow morning in the shed at the bottom of our garden,' said Peter. 'I hope you've got your badge, and that your awful sister Susie hasn't found it and taken it.'

'I've got it on,' said Jack, with a grin. 'And I wear it on my pyjamas at night, so it's always safe. I say, Peter – what's the password?'

'*I* can tell you!' said a voice from up a near-by tree. The boys looked up to see Susie's laughing face looking down at them.

'You don't know it!' said Jack fiercely.

'I do, I do!' said the annoying Susie. 'But I

shan't tell you, and you won't be allowed in at the meeting. What a joke!'

Peter rode off to the rest of the Seven. That Susie! She really was the most AGGRAVATING girl in the whole world!

2 A dreadful blow

Next morning Peter and Janet began preparing for the meeting. Meetings weren't proper meetings, somehow, unless there was plenty to eat and drink while they talked. Their mother was always generous in giving cakes or biscuits and lemonade, and the two children went to find her.

'Hello,' she said, looking up from chopping parsley on a board. 'What are you two after now?'

'We're going to have a Secret Seven meeting,' explained Peter, 'and we wanted something to eat and drink.'

'Well now, let me see – you can have that tin of ginger biscuits – they've gone soft,' said Mummy smiling. 'And you can make yourself some real lemonade – there are plenty of lemons and sugar in the larder.'

'Ooh, good!' said Janet. 'I'll do that. I'll make it with hot water, and let it go cool. Anything else we can have?'

'Jam-tarts,' said Mummy, chopping away hard

at the parsley. 'Only four though, I'm afraid. That's all that were left from supper last night.'

'Four – well, we'll halve them,' said Peter. 'There'll be one half over, so . . .'

'Woof! woof!' said Scamper, at once. The children laughed.

'All right, you shall have the half left over,' said Peter. 'You never miss a word of what we say, do you, Scamper?'

Janet made the lemonade, and Peter got the tin of biscuits and found the tarts. He cut them carefully into exact halves and put them on a plate.

'Come on, Janet,' he said. 'It's nearly half-past ten.'

'Peter, please do tell me the password!' said Janet. 'I'm very, very sorry I've forgotten it.'

'No. I shan't tell you,' said Peter. 'You'll have to be in the shed, anyhow, and you can jolly well listen to the others coming along and saying the password, and feel ashamed of yourself!'

'You're mean!' said Janet. 'Isn't he mean, Scamper?'

Scamper didn't answer. 'There,' said Peter, 'he won't say I'm mean. He never will. Do come on, Janet. I'm not going to wait a minute longer.'

Janet was ready. She put the jug of lemonade and seven unbreakable mugs on an old tray and followed Peter out of the kitchen. 'Thanks, Mummy!' she said, as she went carefully down the steps outside the kitchen door.

Peter was ahead of her. He went along the path that wound between the bushes right down to the bottom of the garden, where the old shed stood that they used for their meetings. On the door was always pinned the sign 'SS'. How many, many times the Secret Seven had met there and made exciting plans!

Janet followed a little way behind, carrying her tray carefully. She suddenly heard Peter give a startled shout, and almost dropped the tray she held.

'What's the matter?' she called and tried to hurry. She came in sight of the shed – and stared in horror.

The door was wide open, and so were the windows. Everything had been turned out of the shed! There were boxes and cushions and sacks, all strewn on the ground in untidy heaps! Whatever had happened?

Janet put her tray down, afraid that she might drop it in her dismay. She looked at Peter in despair.

'Who's done this? Just as we were going to have a meeting too! It's too bad.'

Peter looked into the shed. It was quite empty, except for the shelves round the sides. He was puzzled.

'Janet – it couldn't be Susie, could it?' he said. 'I mean, this is an awful thing to do, throw everything out of our shed. I don't think even Susie would do that.'

'She might,' said Janet, almost in tears. 'Oh, our lovely meeting-place!'

'Here come the others,' said Peter, as Pamela and Barbara appeared down the path together. They stared in amazement at the untidy mess on the ground.

'What's happened?' said Barbara. 'Are we too early?'

'No. We've only *just* seen all this ourselves,' said Peter. 'Hello – here's Jack. Jack, look here.'

'Gosh!' said Jack. 'Who's done this? It can't be Susie. She's been with me all morning till I left just now.'

Colin and George came up just then, and the seven looked ruefully at the boxes and cushions thrown out so untidily. 'We'd better put them back,' said Janet. 'And we'll find out who's done all this to our secret meeting-place.'

They began to put everything back, and then they heard footsteps coming along down the path. Who was it? Peter looked to see.

It was the gardener, carrying a strong broom over his shoulder, a pail of water in his hand, and some cloths hanging on the side of the pail. He stared at the seven in annoyance.

'Hey, you! What are you doing? I've only just thrown all that rubbish out!'

'But why?' demanded Peter, indignantly. 'This shed is our meeting-place, and this isn't rubbish. We use it.'

'Oh, well, I don't know anything about that,' said the gardener. 'All I know is that your father told me to clear out this place, burn all the rubbish, and do a spot of painting. He said it was going to rack and ruin, and he wanted it cleaned up.'

'I see,' said Peter, his heart sinking. If his father had planned this, there was nothing to be done. He turned to the others. 'Come on, let's find somewhere to talk,' he said. 'We can't meet in our shed for a while, that's certain. How annoying!'

'Never mind! We'll think of somewhere just as good,' said Colin. But nobody agreed with him. They thought the shed was the finest place in the world for Secret Seven meetings!

The Seven, followed by Scamper with his tail well down, went slowly up the garden path. Somehow it seemed dreadful not to have their usual meeting-place.

'We'll go to the summer-house,' said Peter. 'Oh, look, there's Mummy, Janet. We'll ask her about the shed.'

'Mummy!' called Janet. 'Why didn't you tell us the shed was going to be cleaned and painted – our own shed, I mean, where we meet? I do think *somebody* might have told us.'

'Oh dear, I quite forgot to tell you that Daddy wanted it cleaned and mended,' said Mummy. 'It was almost falling to bits here and there, you know. But you can have it for a meeting-place again when it's finished. It will look nice and bright and clean then.'

'But we like it old and dark and untidy,' said Peter mournfully. 'And I do think it's a pity to have it done in the holidays, Mummy, just when we want to use it.'

'Yes, I agree that that's a pity,' said Mummy, looking very sorry. 'I would have stopped it if I'd known that it was to be done just now. Well – you'll have to find another meeting-place. What about the attic?'

'Oh no,' said Janet. 'It's no fun meeting in a

house, Mummy, with other people in near-by rooms. We want a secret, lonely place, we do really.'

'Yes . . . I suppose you do,' said Mummy. 'Well, I can't suggest one, I'm afraid. Go to the summer-house just for now.'

'We were going to,' said Peter, still very doleful. Soon they were all squashed into the little old summer-house. They didn't much like it, because it was rather earwiggy.

They began to eat the ginger biscuits. 'Rather soft, I'm afraid,' said Janet.

'Oh, I like them soft and squidgy,' said Pam. 'I hate them when you have to bite so hard they splinter in your mouth. Hey, this is good lemonade! Did your mother make it, Janet?'

'No. I made it myself,' said Janet proudly. 'Peter, hadn't we better talk about where to have a new meeting-place?'

'Yes,' said Peter. 'And I vote that we all of us have a good hunt round to find somewhere, some absolutely secret place that even Jack's sister Susie won't find. It mustn't be too far away. I'll give you today to find one. Meet here this evening, in this summer-house again, at six o'clock.'

'Right,' said Colin. 'I think I know of one already.'

'Well, don't tell us now,' said Peter. 'We'll each give in our ideas this evening and put it to the vote to see which is the best. We must do these things properly.'

'Yes,' said everyone, and took a drink of Janet's lemonade.

'What about the password?' said Jack. 'We were all so upset about the shed that we never even gave the password.'

'We've all got our badges on,' said Pamela. 'I had an awful hunt for mine. I put it in such a safe place that it was almost too safe for me to find!'

'Where was it?' asked George.

'I buried it in the pot of maidenhair fern my mother has in the drawing-room,' said Pam, with a giggle. 'And then forgot about it. It took me ages to remember it.'

'I thought it looked a bit grubby,' said Peter. 'I think that's a silly place.'

'Oh, I wrapped it in paper,' said Pam. 'But I forgot that Mummy watered it twice a week – so, of course, the paper soaked off and made my badge messy.'

'It's a good thing it didn't put out roots and grow!' said Peter. Everyone laughed.

'Peter, could we have a new password?' said Jack. 'Susie knows our last one. I'm most dreadfully sorry, and I don't know how she knew it, unless she hung round our last meeting and heard it.'

'All right. We'll choose a new one,' said Peter. 'It's time we did, anyway. I must say that your sister Susie is getting worse and worse, Jack. I hope she's nowhere about just now.'

Jack got up and went out of the summer-house. 'Nobody's anywhere near,' he said. 'Quick – what's the new password?'

'Easter-egg,' said Peter. 'That's easy to remember, because it's the Easter holidays.'

'Easter-egg,' repeated everyone, in low voices. Pam took out a notebook and began to write it down.

'Don't *you* write it down, Jack!' said Janet, 'or Susie will find it. I wonder how she knew our last password?'

'Well, she called out, "Your password is Sugar-mouse" just as I was leaving,' said Jack. 'And I don't mind owning up now that I was really glad to hear it, because I'd forgotten it completely.'

'Sugar-mouse!' said Peter, in astonishment. 'It was nothing of the sort. Susie just made that up because she knew you'd forgotten it. She hoped you would rap on the door of the shed and yell out "Sugar-mouse" and make a fool of yourself.'

Jack went red. 'What was the password then?' he said. 'Janet, you tell me. Peter won't.'

Janet went red too. '*I've* forgotten it as well,' she said.

Pam blushed as red as Janet, so Peter knew she had forgotten too! He rapped on the summer-house table.

'The last password was a very simple one,' he said. 'It was "Thursday". Just that, "Thursday".'

'Gosh, so it was,' said Barbara. 'I just couldn't remember if it was "Thursday" or "Friday".'

'*I* thought it was Sunday,' said Colin, with a laugh. 'It was a silly password to choose, Peter, too easy to muddle up with the other days of the week. "Easter-egg" is much better.'

'Well, let's hope that Barbara and Colin don't mix it up with "Christmas present" or "Birthday gift"!' said Peter. 'Now – we've eaten everything, and Scamper's had his half-tart, and we've drunk all the lemonade – what about separating and hunting for a new meeting-place?'

'Right,' said everyone and got up. They all went off up the path to the front gate, and most of them were murmuring two words to themselves as they went.

'Easter-egg! Easter-egg! I must remember Easter-egg!'

3 Plenty of ideas

At six o'clock that evening there was a continual noise of footsteps up the path to the little summer-house. Janet, Peter, and Scamper were inside, waiting.

'Easter-egg,' said Jack, walking inside. There was no door, for the summer-house was three-sided, with its fourth side open to the garden.

'Easter-egg,' said Barbara, walking in, too.

'Where's your badge?' asked Peter sharply.

'Oh – I've got it, it's all right,' said Barbara, feeling in her pocket. 'I don't know why I forgot to pin it on.' She pinned it on carefully and sat down.

The other three came along, each solemnly giving the password.

'For once nobody *yelled* it out,' said Peter. He took a notebook out of his pocket, and licked his pencil. 'Now then. I want your reports on any likely places to meet secretly. Colin, you begin.'

'Well, there's a fine big tree at the bottom of our garden,' began Colin hopefully. 'It's a great chestnut, and . . .'

'No good, I'm afraid,' said Peter, 'but I'll put it down. It would hardly be a secret meeting-place! Everyone would see us going down the garden to it, and people passing the wall nearby would hear us up there. Barbara, what's *your* idea?'

'Oh, it's a silly one,' said Barbara. 'There's an old hut in a field nearby our house, and . . .'

'I know it,' said Peter, scribbling in his notebook. 'Not a bad idea, Barbara. You, Pam?'

'I simply haven't any idea at all,' said Pam. 'I've thought and thought, but it's no use.'

'*Not* very helpful,' said Peter, putting a cross against Pam's name in his notebook. 'You, George?'

'Well, there's an empty caravan in a field not far from here,' said George. 'I know who owns it – it's a friend of my father's. I think I could get permission for us to use it.'

This sounded exciting. Everyone looked admiringly at George, who seemed quite pleased with himself.

'You, Jack?' said Peter. 'And don't suggest anywhere near *your* house, because of Susie.'

'I'm not going to,' said Jack. 'I'm not quite so silly as that. I've chosen somewhere a long way away, down by the river. It's an old boathouse that nobody ever uses.'

This sounded exciting too. Peter wrote it down solemnly. 'Now we've heard everyone's idea except mine and Janet's. We went out hunting together, and Scamper came too – and we've all got the same idea.'

'What?' asked everyone.

'Well, it's a cave in the quarry near the field where we grow potatoes,' said Peter. 'So it's on my father's farm, and not very far. It's absolutely lonely and secret, and goes back into the hill behind the quarry. Scamper found it, actually.'

'That sounds good – a secret cave,' said Pam.

'Well, we'll now put all our ideas to the vote,' said Peter, and handed round slips of paper. 'Please write down on these papers what ideas you like best – but nobody must vote for their own idea, of course. I'll just go shortly over them again:

'Colin suggests a tree, but it's not a very *secret* place. Barbara suggested that old hut in the field near her house – but the roof's almost off and the rain would come in. Pam has no ideas. George suggests the caravan owned by his father's friend, a very good idea, but I don't honestly think we'd be allowed to use it because it's still furnished. I'd be afraid of breaking something.'

Peter paused for breath. 'Jack suggested the old boathouse by the river. Fine – but isn't it rather far away for a meeting-place? It's at least a mile away. And you know what Janet and I suggest – the cave. But that isn't a really comfortable place. There you are – please vote on your papers, fold them in half, and give them to me.'

Everyone solemnly wrote something on their papers, then handed them to Peter. He opened them and read them. When he looked up, his eyes were shining with pleasure.

'Er – well – it's very funny, but everyone except me and Janet have voted for the cave. We couldn't vote for our own idea, of course. So it's five votes for the cave – and the cave it will be. I'm glad – it's a great place really!'

'Is it? Let's go and see it straight away!' said Jack. 'It's not very far.'

'All right, come on then,' said Peter. 'We'll have a quick look, and then plan what to bring to it tomorrow. We'll settle into it at once.'

This was exciting. They all got up and went out

into the bright sunshine. It was almost half-past six, and as warm as could be.

'This way,' said Peter, and led the way down his garden and through a gate into a field. His father owned the farmland at the back of the house, and it stretched away over the hills, the fields green with growing corn and root-crops.

Peter took them down a grassy path, past a pond with ducks on it, and then turned to the right towards the old quarry. Sand had been dug from it years ago, and it had then been abandoned. They all filed into the quarry and looked round.

Scamper ran in front. 'He'll show you,' said Peter. 'Just as he showed me and Janet this morning!' Scamper ran up to what looked like a rabbit path, over a little sandy hill, then down into a hollow behind. The others followed. Scamper stood waiting for them, his tail waving to and fro.

He ran through a gap in some thick bushes and disappeared. The others went through the gap too and looked for Scamper. He had gone!

'He's gone into the cave,' said Peter, grinning. 'You can see the entrance just there. It's all hung over with some plant that has sent long, trailing stems down, and has almost hidden the entrance to the cave. Come on – it's really quite exciting!'

4   In the cave

The Secret Seven crowded together to see the cave. There was no proper path to it, and they had to squeeze through close-growing bushes of bright yellow broom to get to it. The bushes grew almost up to the cave entrance.

'No wonder Janet and I never spotted this cave before,' said Peter. 'We've been in this old sand quarry heaps of times, but never found the cave. It was only because old Scamper disappeared and we went to look for him that we found it. We were standing here, calling him, when he suddenly appeared under the trailing leaves that hide the cave! Didn't you, Scamper?'

'Woof!' said Scamper, and ran into the cave and back, as if to say, 'Do come on, it's a fine place!'

The trailing stems that hung down over the entrance certainly hid it very well. Peter pulled the greenery aside. 'It's like a curtain,' he said. 'Look – now you can see into the cave properly.'

Everyone bent their heads and looked in. It certainly was a fine cave!

'Nice and big, and with a lovely sandy floor!' said Jack. 'I don't see why you said it's not comfortable, Peter. Sand is lovely to sit on.'

'Oh well, I had to say *something* against it, as it was Janet's suggestion and mine,' said Peter.

By now they were all in the cave. Pam flung herself down on the sand. It was very soft indeed.

'Lovely!' she said. 'I'd like to sleep here in this sand. I could burrow my body down into it and make a lovely bed. It's a *wonderful* meeting-place, I think.'

'Nobody would EVER find it!' said George, looking round. 'It's a bit dark, that's the only thing. It's that green curtain over the entrance that makes it so dark.'

Janet obligingly held the curtain back, and the sun streamed into the cave.

'Fine!' said Colin. 'We can have the curtain back when we're just playing about, and draw it when we're having a secret meeting. Couldn't be better. A cave with a ready-made curtain!'

'And look, the cave has a rock roof, all uneven, high here and low there,' said Barbara. 'And there are rocky shelves round the walls; we can use those to put our things on. We'll bring all kinds of things here! I expect we'll have to use this cave all the Easter hols, so we'll make it a kind of home as well as a meeting-place. Shall we?'

Everyone thought this was a very good idea. 'We'll bring the shed cushions here,' said Janet. 'And a box for a table.'

'And keep food here, and lemonade or orangeade,' said Jack. 'Won't it be fun?'

'Yes, and you'll have to be careful not to let Susie follow you here,' said Peter warningly. 'She'd just love to come here and mess things about, bring her silly, giggling friends with her too, I expect, and have a picnic or something in the middle of the cave.'

'I'll be very careful,' promised Jack. 'Well, I must say this is a brilliant place for the Secret Seven. Not too far away, perfectly secret, quite lonely, and our very own. Can any of us come here when we like, Peter? When there's not a meeting or anything planned? I'd love to come and read here by myself.'

'Yes. I don't see why this shouldn't be a kind of headquarters as well as a meeting-place,' said Peter. 'Anyone can come whenever they like, but please leave it tidy, and don't go and eat all the food we leave here!'

'Of course not,' said everyone at once.

'If we come alone and want something to eat we'll bring it ourselves,' said Colin, and everyone agreed.

'Now, let's see. We'll come tomorrow at half-past ten,' began Peter, but Jack interrupted before he could say any more.

'Oh, earlier than that, Peter! It's going to be fun; I'd like to come earlier. Can't we make it half-past nine?'

'No, because Janet and I have jobs to do for our father and mother,' said Peter. 'We'll say ten, if you like. We can get our jobs done by then, I expect.'

'I've got jobs to do as well,' said Pam. 'I always help Mother with the housework in the hols. So does Barbara.'

'Well, say ten,' repeated Peter. 'And bring what you can to make the cave comfortable and homely. Bring books if you like – the cave's quite dry – and games.'

Everyone was sorry to leave the exciting cave. It really was a nice one, spacious, though the roof was not very high, and it was only in places that the Seven could stand upright – clean, with its floor of soft sand – and reaching back into a very nice, mysterious darkness, quite out of reach of the sunshine.

Peter held back the curtain of greenery till everyone had gone out. Then he let it drop into place and arranged it so that hardly a bit of the entrance showed. Nobody at all would ever guess there was a big cave behind it, going right into the hill beyond!

Scamper came out last of all, his tail wagging madly. He liked the cave. It was exciting. There was no smell of rabbits in it, which was disappointing, but it was good fun to pretend there was, and to scrabble hard at the sand with his front paws, and send it showering into the air!

The Seven all walked back to the gate at the bottom of Peter's garden, and then up the garden to the front gate. They said goodbye, and went off to their different homes, thinking exciting thoughts.

Susie met Jack as he came in, and looked at his sandy shoes.

'Where have you been?' she demanded. 'I've been looking for you everywhere. Where did you get that sand on your shoes?'

'Ask no questions, and I'll tell you no lies,' said Jack, pushing by her.

'You've been with the Secret Seven, I know you have,' said Susie, and she laughed. 'What's

the password? Is it still Sugar-mouse? Ha, ha – I
tricked you nicely over that, didn't I?'

5 Settling in

Next day Peter and Janet felt very excited. They went down the garden to collect the old cushions they had had in the shed. The gardener had put them into another shed, together with the boxes, sacks, and other things.

He was very busy repairing the old shed. The two children peeped inside. It would certainly be nice and clean when it was all finished.

'I'd rather have the cave for the holidays though,' said Peter, and Janet nodded.

They were very laden indeed as they made their way down to the quarry. Scamper carried a bone in his mouth. He knew quite well they were going to the cave, and he wanted to take something too!

Peter and Janet were there before the others. They drew aside the curtain of greenery and went in. The curtain fell behind them.

'Don't draw it back yet, till the others come,' said Peter. 'They'll have to give the password outside the curtain before we pull it back. Otherwise we'd never know who was coming in! But the password will tell us it's the Secret Seven.'

Janet set down the cushions. Peter put down the box he had brought. It was heavy, because he had filled it with all kinds of things. He began to unpack.

'Hand me the things,' said Janet. 'I'll arrange them nicely on these rocky shelves. There's no hole we can use for a cupboard, but that won't matter. Gosh, isn't this going to be fun?'

Peter looked at his watch. 'It's almost ten,' he said. 'You go on arranging things, and I'll wait just at the entrance, behind the curtain, and ask for the passwords. The sand outside is so soft that we shan't hear anyone coming. I must watch for them.'

Almost immediately there came a soft shuffle outside. 'Password,' said Peter, in a low voice.

'Easter-egg!' said Colin's voice. Peter pulled aside the curtain of greenery, and Colin came staggering in, carrying a big cardboard box. He collapsed on the soft, sandy floor.

'Gosh! I never knew books were so heavy! I've brought my whole set of "Famous Five" books to put on the shelves for anyone to borrow, and they've nearly dragged my arms out!'

'Oh, fine, there's one I want to read again,' said Peter, pleased. 'Find a nice even shelf of rock somewhere along the wall there, Colin, and put the books up neatly.'

A small cough came from outside the cave. Someone was waiting to be allowed in. 'Password!' said Peter, at once.

'Easter-egg!' said two voices together, and Peter lifted the green curtain. In came Pam and Barbara carrying parcels.

'Janet will see to those,' said Peter, taking up his post by the curtain again. Soon he heard the soft sound of feet coming quietly over the sand outside, and heard, too, the noise of people squeezing through the thick bushes of yellow broom.

Password!' he said, and two voices answered together. 'Easter-egg!'

'Not so loud, idiots!' said Peter, and pulled aside the green curtain, grinning widely at Jack and George. He peered cautiously behind them.

'It's all right. I slipped off while Susie was at the bottom of our garden,' said Jack, staggering in. 'I've brought two bottles of juice and two bottles

of water. Mother said I could, as her share towards the Secret Seven goings-on!'

'Goodo!' said Peter, pleased. He drew back the
curtain and tied it with a bit of string, so that
the sunshine flooded into the cave. He looked
all round outside to make sure that no one was
about.

'I think we're absolutely safe and secret here,'
he said. 'This quarry has been deserted for years,
and I don't expect anyone remembers there was
ever a cave here.'

'Scamper would bark if anyone wandered
near,' said Janet. 'Then we could quickly pull the
curtain over the entrance and lie as quiet as anything!'

'Yes. Scamper would certainly warn us,' said
Peter. 'Now, how are you all getting on?'

The cave was beginning to look quite cosy and
furnished. The box-table was in the middle.
Cushions were here and there on the sandy floor,
ready for anyone to sit on. Arranged on the
uneven ledges of the rocky wall were Colin's
books and some of Jack's. Plastic cups had been
neatly put in a row by Janet, and on a wider ledge
she had put Jack's bottles.

A tin stood in one corner. It had in it some of the

food that the Seven had brought, and on another ledge stood a tin of boiled sweets, a packet of oatmeal biscuits, and two bars of chocolate brought by Pam. A small jar of potted crab paste stood next to a jar of home-made strawberry jam.

'It all looks very good,' said Peter approvingly. 'Very good indeed.'

'Yes. We've found places for everything,' said Janet, pleased. 'That corner over there belongs to Scamper, by the way, that's where he's buried the big bone he brought with him. Please don't disturb it, anyone. You can stop sitting on it, Scamper. I've told everyone it's your own special corner.'

Scamper still sat there, however. To him a bone was a very precious possession indeed, and he had to make *quite* sure that everyone understood it was *his* bone.

'I'm hungry after all this,' announced Jack, 'I vote we choose something to eat. We've got very well-filled cupboards!'

'I'll have a ginger bun,' said Colin. 'My mother made them yesterday. They're lovely. Let's begin with those.'

So there they sat, all the Secret Seven, happily munching ginger buns. The sun streamed in at the cave entrance, for the green curtain was still pulled back. What a lovely meeting-place – the best they had ever had!

6 Jack is very puzzled

The cave was a great success. On rainy days it was a wonderful place to lie in and read, or play games. Each of the seven burrowed into the sand and made his or her own bed or hole. Each had a cushion for their head. The shelves were always kept stacked with papers and magazines, and with food and drink.

'We couldn't have found a better place,' said Colin. 'Jack, does Susie ever bother about where you disappear to for hours on end?'

'Goodness, yes,' said Jack. 'She keeps on and on about it. She knows our old shed is no longer a meeting-place, because she went to have a look at it. I have to be awfully careful not to let her follow me when I come here. Yesterday I turned round and there she was, keeping to the bushes beside the road, hoping I wouldn't see her.'

'What did you do?' asked Pam.

'I turned a corner and went off to the sweet shop instead of coming here,' said Jack. 'I do hope she won't find our cave.'

'Let's go into the quarry and play hide-and-seek,' said Janet, getting up. 'The sun's out again, and I'm longing to stretch my legs.'

So off they all went. Jack was chosen to shut his eyes and count a hundred before he began looking. The cave was to be Home.

Jack stood by a tree at the other side of the quarry, counting nice and slowly. When he had counted a hundred, he looked round. Could he see anyone behind a bush, or lying in the lush grass nearby?

No – not one of the others was to be seen. He moved cautiously round his tree, keeping his eyes open for a sudden movement somewhere.

He glanced towards the cave, which he could just see between a gap in the broom bushes that hid it so well. Then he stared. Someone was slipping into the cave! Who was it? He just couldn't see.

That's not fair, thought Jack. They haven't given me a chance to find them. Well, I'll soon find out which of the seven it is, and tell them what I think of them!

He saw a patch of blue nearby and recognised Pam's dress behind a bush. He rushed at her, but she escaped and ran squealing to the cave.

Then he found Barbara, Janet, and Scamper together, crouching behind a great hummock of sand. He ran to catch them and fell headlong over a tuft of grass. They rushed away, the girls squealing and Scamper barking.

He nearly caught Colin behind a tree, but Colin was too quick for him. Let's see – that only leaves one more, said Jack to himself. The first one I saw going into the cave – then the three girls – then Colin – myself – and so there's just one more. It's Peter or George.

He hunted here and there, and then suddenly fell over two giggling boys. It was Peter and George, half-buried in the soft sand. Jack grabbed at Peter and caught him, but George escaped to the cave.

'I'm caught all right!' said Peter, grinning. 'I'll be "He" next. Let's call out to everyone in the cave.'

'Wait a minute,' said Jack, looking puzzled. 'There's something I don't understand. Let's go up to the cave.'

Peter went with him to the cave, where the other five were waiting.

'What don't you understand?' asked Peter.

'Well, listen – first I saw someone slipping into the cave immediately after I'd finished counting,' said Jack, 'which wasn't really fair. Then I found Pam, then Janet and Barbara, then Colin, then you and George, Peter.'

'Well – what's puzzling you?' asked Peter.

'Just this – that makes *eight* of us, not counting Scamper,' said Jack. 'And what I want to know is, who was the eighth?'

They all counted. Yes, Jack was right. That made eight, not seven. Everyone said at once that they hadn't slipped into the cave before Jack discovered them.

'Well, who was that first person then, if it wasn't any of us?' said Jack, really puzzled. 'I tell you I saw somebody go into the cave before I discovered *any* of you. Who was it?'

Everyone began to look round uneasily. Peter pulled the green curtain back as far as he could, and the sunshine filled the cave, except for the dark places at the back.

'There's nobody here,' said Pam. 'Oh, Jack, do you suppose it could have been Susie?'

'I don't know. I only just saw *somebody*, but I haven't any idea who it was,' said Jack. 'And look here, surely that somebody must still be in here! I found Pam almost immediately, and she rushed off to the cave. You didn't see anyone here, did you, Pam?'

'Of course not,' said Pam. 'If I'd seen Susie I would have been furious with her!'

Peter took down a torch from the shelf of rock nearby and switched it on. He flashed it towards the dark corners at the end of the cave. 'Come forth!' he said, in a hollow voice. 'Come forth, O wicked intruder!'

But nobody came. The far corners of the cave, now lit brilliantly by the torch, were quite empty.

'It's odd,' said Jack, frowning. 'Very odd. Give me the torch, Peter. I'll go and see if there's any corner or hole at the end of the cave that we haven't noticed.'

'Well, there isn't,' said Peter, giving him the torch. 'Janet and I had a good look when we first found the cave!'

All the same, Jack went to the far end and had a very good look round, flashing the torch everywhere. There seemed to be nowhere that anyone could hide.

He came back, still looking puzzled. 'Cheer up,' said Peter. 'You must have imagined someone, Jack. Anyway, *would* anyone come to that cave while we were all of us here, in plain view?'

'But that's just what we were not,' said Jack. 'We were playing hide-and-seek, and there wasn't a sound, and all of us, except me, were well hidden. Anybody coming here just then would not have heard or seen anything of us. They would have thought the place deserted.'

'Yes. I see what you mean,' said Peter. 'All the same, there's nobody here. So cheer up, Jack, and let's go on with the game. My turn to find you all. Go and hide!'

7 A real mystery

Nobody said any more about Jack's idea that someone had slipped into the cave. Jack began to think he really must have imagined it. Perhaps it was a shadow from a cloud or something? They all played the game of hide-and-seek again and again, and nobody saw mysterious people slipping into the cave any more!

'It's time to tidy up and go home,' said Peter, at last. 'What a mess we seem to make when we've been in the cave for even a short time!'

The girls shook up the cushions, and the boys gathered up the rubbish and put it into a bag to take home. Then Janet put the rest of the food back on the shelves, and tidied up Colin's set of 'Five' books.

'There!' she said. 'Everything tidy! If our mothers came and looked in they would be most astonished.'

They all laughed. They went out of the cave, and Peter pulled the green curtain carefully across. Then off they went home.

'Same time tomorrow!' called Peter, when they all said goodbye to him and Janet and Scamper at his front gate.

'No! You've forgotten – we're all going to bike over to Penton and see the circus come through,' said Colin. 'We're meeting at eleven at my house.'

'Oh, yes, how could I forget!' said Peter. 'We'll go to the cave after dinner tomorrow afternoon.'

Next day they had a good morning, watching the long circus procession passing through the little town of Penton. Then they biked back for their dinners, and, at various times, set off to the cave.

Pam and Barbara arrived first, Pam, very pleased because her granny had given her a tin of peppermints for the Secret Seven to enjoy.

'I'll put them beside the other tins,' she said. 'Hello – look, Barbara, there's a tin on the floor of the cave. Who do you suppose knocked that down? We're the first here today!'

'Perhaps it overbalanced,' said Barbara.

'And gosh, look – we left a whole bar of chocolate, a very big one, just *here*,' said Pam. 'I put it there myself. That's gone!'

'It's probably somewhere else,' said Barbara. Then she herself noticed something. 'Gosh, look

– three of our cushions are missing! Has some-body been here?'

'It's Susie,' said Pam frowning. 'That's who it is. She didn't come with us to Penton today, so she must have come here instead! She has fol-lowed Jack sometime or other, and found out our meeting-place. Bother Susie!'

'Here are the others,' said Barbara. 'Let's tell them.'

They heard the password murmured outside the cave. 'Easter-egg' – then the curtain was pushed aside and in came Colin and George.

'Susie's been here!' said Pam angrily. 'Look, there are cushions missing, and our big bar of chocolate is gone, and a tin was on the ground.'

'And look, those currant buns we were saving for today are nearly all gone!' said Barbara, open-ing a tin. 'Would you believe it!'

Soon Peter, Janet, and Jack arrived and were also told the news. 'But it needn't have been Susie,' said Peter, trying to be fair, though he felt perfectly certain it was. 'It could quite well have been a tramp.'

'He'd have taken lots more things,' said Pam. 'And what would he want with *cushions*! We might meet him down a lane carrying them, and we'd know he was the thief at once. No tramp would be as silly as that.'

'That's true,' said Peter. 'Well, Jack, you'll have to find out if it's Susie.'

'All right,' said Jack, looking troubled. 'I'll go now. But somehow I don't think it *is* Susie, you know. I can't help remembering that person, whoever it was, that I saw slipping into the cave yesterday.'

Jack went off to find Susie. The others each took a peppermint from the tin that Pam offered them, and settled down to read. Colin finished his book and went to get another. He gave an exclamation.

'One of my "Famous Five" books has gone! Has anyone borrowed it? It's *Five go down to the sea.*'

Nobody had. 'I know it's not Jack,' said Colin. 'He's just finished reading it. Well, if that's Susie again I'll have something to say to her!'

Jack came back in about an hour. 'Easter-egg' he said, outside the cave, and Peter called him in.

'Well,' he said, throwing himself down on the sandy floor. 'I've had an awful time. Susie says she's never been *near* our new meeting-place, she says she doesn't even know where it is! She flew into such a temper when I accused her of coming and taking things, that Mother heard her, and came to see what was the matter.'

'Oh, bother!' said Peter. 'You might have kept your mother out of this. What happened next?'

'Mother made me tell where our meeting-place is,' said poor Jack, looking really miserable. 'I couldn't help it, Peter, really I couldn't. She *made* me.'

There was silence. Everyone knew that it was wrong, and also quite impossible, to refuse to tell mothers anything they wanted to know. But to give away their wonderful new meeting-place! How truly shocking.

'Was Susie there when you told?' asked Peter.

'Yes,' said Jack. 'She was, and she said she was jolly well coming to find the cave and make a real mess of it! I don't think she did come here this morning. She was with Jeff all the time in the garden. Mother said so.'

'Well then, who did?' said Peter, puzzled. 'It's a strange thief who comes and takes three *cushions*!'

There was a silence. Pam glanced round the cave fearfully. Who was it who came here? Jack had seen someone yesterday, and now the someone had come again today. WHO was it?

'Now that Susie knows about our cave, I think

that someone must be here on guard whenever we're not here,' said Peter. 'I mean – we can't let Susie come and mess everything up. I can quite see that if it wasn't her who came and took the things this morning, she must be really furious with us for thinking it was.'

'I wouldn't be surprised if she brought Jeff with her and turned the whole place upside down now,' said Jack gloomily. 'You don't know Susie like I do.'

'Well, let's make things jolly unpleasant for them if they *do* come,' said George. 'Let's balance a jug of water on that ledge over the green curtain. As soon as the curtain is moved, the jug will overbalance and pour water all over them.'

Pam giggled. 'Yes. Let's do that!'

'And let's do what my cousin once did to someone he didn't like,' said Colin. 'He got a reel of cotton and wound it all over and across the entrance to our summer-house – and he dipped it in honey first! Then when this awful boy walked into the summer-house, he walked right through the sticky threads and thought that an enormous spider's web had caught him!'

'How horrible!' said Pam, shuddering. 'To have sticky thread all over you like that!'

'Susie would hate it,' said Barbara. 'She loathes

getting caught in spider thread. But who's got cotton or honey? Nobody here!'

'I can run indoors and get a reel of silk from my work-box,' said Janet, 'and there's some honey in a jar in our kitchen, I know. But aren't we being rather horrid to Susie?'

'No, Susie will only get caught in our tricks if she finds the cave and comes to turn it upside down,' said Pam. 'It will be her own fault if she gets caught. Nobody else's.'

'It's no good being soft-hearted with Susie,' said Jack gloomily. 'Actually, sometimes I think she's cleverer than any of us!'

Janet ran off to get the honey and the reel of silk. Barbara complained because her cushion was gone and she now had nothing to rest her head on.

'I suppose whoever took our cushions did it for some kind of silly joke,' she said. 'And probably threw them into the bushes somewhere.'

'I'll go and look,' said Colin, and got up. But the cushions were nowhere to be seen, and he soon came back. Janet came with him, having got the reel and the honey.

'We'll get the tricks ready when we go home to tea,' said Peter. 'I'll slip up after tea to make sure that no one's been into the cave, and I'll come last thing at night too.'

Just before they left they arranged the booby-traps. Janet ran the grey silk thread through the sticky honey, and the boys wound it back and forth across the entrance to the cave, twisting it round the plants that lined the edges of the cave entrance from top to bottom.

'There!' said Peter, at last. 'No one can get in without getting covered with thin, sticky threads! And what a shock they'll get too, when they draw back the curtain and get swamped with water from that jug! I've balanced it very carefully, so that at the slightest pulling back of the green curtain the water will pour out!'

Everyone giggled and wished they could be there to see the booby-traps catch any intruder. 'I hope Jeff comes with Susie, I can't bear him,' said Jack. 'And shan't I laugh if Susie comes back sticky and wet! Come on, let's go.'

After tea Peter went up to the cave to examine the booby-traps. They were still there! The jug of water, half-hidden by leaves, was still in place, and he could see the grey, sticky threads gleaming behind the green curtain.

'Susie and Jeff haven't been yet,' he told Janet, when he got back. 'I'll slip up again just before it gets dark and have another look.'

So up he went once more to the cave, but again

the booby-traps were still there, untouched. Susie won't come now, he thought. I'll be up here before nine o'clock tomorrow morning and watch out for her in case she comes then.

8 Scamper is a help

Jack came to see Peter just before nine next day. 'I came to tell you that Susie's not been near the cave,' he told Peter. 'I kept an eye on her all yesterday evening and this morning. She's gone off to her music lesson now, so we're safe till twelve o'clock anyhow.'

'Right,' said Peter. 'Well, help me with the few jobs I have to do, and then we'll go up with Janet and Scamper. We'll try to get there just before the others come.'

So at five to ten, Peter, Janet, Scamper, and Jack made their way to the quarry and then up to the cave.

They looked up to where the jug was so carefully balanced on a ledge, and grinned.

'I'll get it,' said Jack, and climbed up to remove it.

'We'll have to break these threads ourselves,' said Janet. 'What a waste of booby-traps, wasn't it? Ooh, be careful, you'll get honey all over you!'

They broke the threads as carefully as possible, so as not to get themselves sticky, and went into the cave. And then they stood there in astonishment, gazing round as if they could not believe their eyes!

The tins were all opened – and emptied! Some were flung on the floor. Two more of the cushions had gone. A bottle of orangeade had disappeared, and so had a bottle of water. The tin of peppermints had completely vanished, and also some more books. A torch that Colin had left on a shelf had gone too.

'But – but – how could anyone get *in*?' stammered Peter, utterly astonished. 'Our booby-traps were still there – those threads were quite unbroken. NOBODY could have come in, and yet look at this. I don't like it. There's something very strange going on in this cave – and I just don't – like – it!'

The three children felt scared. It was quite clear that *no one* had gone into the cave, because the sticky silk threads would certainly have been broken. But how could their belongings have been taken, and their tins emptied, if no one had been in the cave?

'You know,' said Jack, looking all round him fearfully, 'you know, Peter, I was quite certain I saw somebody slipping into the cave that time we played hide-and-seek. You kept saying I must have imagined it, but I didn't.'

'Well, certainly *somebody's* about, somebody who likes eating and drinking,' said Peter. 'And if he didn't get into our cave from the *outside*, he must know a way in from the *inside*!'

'But that's silly too,' said Janet. 'We know there's no way into the cave from the inside. We've had a jolly good look.'

'Scamper seems very interested in the cave this morning,' said Jack. 'Look at him sniffing and nosing round.'

Scamper certainly was interested. He ran here and there excitedly, giving little barks and whimpers, as if to say, 'I could tell you such a lot if only I could speak!'

He ran over to the place where he had buried his bone, dug it up, and carefully took it to another corner and buried it there. Peter laughed.

'He's afraid our visitor might find his bone – see how deep he's burying it this time! Hey, Scamper, you're sending sand all over us!'

Janet looked round at the untidy cave with its empty tins and scattered books. Tears came into her eyes. 'I made it all so nice,' she said. 'And we had such a lot of good food here. Who is this horrible visitor who comes when we're not here and steals like this? Where does he come from? How does he get here if he doesn't come in at the entrance?'

'Let's look all round the cave again, very, very carefully to see if there's another entrance some-where,' said Jack. 'There might be a small hole that someone could wriggle through, covered with sand.'

They looked thoroughly, Scamper sniffing too. But no, no matter how Scamper sniffed all round and about, or how the children dug here and there to find a hole under the rocky walls, nothing was found that would help to solve the mystery.

'And a very strange mystery it is too,' said Peter. 'I said I didn't like it, and I don't. I vote we clear up this cave and find another meeting-place. It's going to be no fun if we keep having our things stolen and messed about by some un-known visitor.'

'Yes. *I* don't feel as if I want to be here any more either,' said Janet. 'It's a shame. It's such a good place. Well, the others will be along soon, so let's just clear up a bit, and we'll tell them when they come.'

It wasn't long before the others came, all four of

them, chattering and laughing as they walked through the old quarry.

As soon as they arrived at the cave, Peter told them what had happened. They stared at his grave face and listened in astonishment to what he told them.

'It's very odd,' said George. 'I don't understand it. Taking food – and cushions – and books! It sounds like someone hiding somewhere and needing food, and something soft to lie on.'

'If one or two of us hid here in the cave tonight, we might see whoever it is that comes,' said Colin.

There was a silence. Nobody liked the idea at all. This mysterious visitor didn't sound a very nice person to lie in wait for.

'Well,' said Peter at last, 'I'm no coward, but considering that there really isn't any place in this cave that we could hide in without being seen almost at once, I don't see much point in your suggestion, Colin. I mean the intruder, whoever he is, would probably see *us* before we spotted him. Anyway, I don't like the sound of him.'

'Nor do I,' said Jack. 'I vote we clear out of here and have another meeting-place. What's the sense of bringing stuff here and having it taken as soon as our back's turned?''

They began to clear up the cave. It was really very sad. Scamper watched them in surprise. Why were they looking so miserable? Why were they packing up everything? Well, he'd certainly better get his bone then! He couldn't leave that behind if everyone was leaving the cave!

He ran over to the corner where he had buried it. His sharp nose sniffed something else not far off on a low ledge of rock. Did it belong to the children? It didn't really smell like any of them. Scamper could always tell what shoe or glove belonged to any of the Seven just by sniffing it!

Scamper sniffed at this thing on the ledge, and then picked it up in his mouth. Perhaps it did belong to one of the children after all. He ran with it to Peter and dropped it at his feet with a little bark.

'Hello, Scamper, what is it?' said Peter. He bent down and picked up a small, dirty notebook with a frayed elastic band round it. 'Anyone own this?' he asked, holding it up.

Nobody did. Jack came up, excited.

'Peter! It might have been dropped by our strange visitor! Look inside!'

Peter slipped off the elastic band and opened the little notebook. His eyes suddenly shone. 'Yes!' he said, in a low voice. 'It *does* belong to our visitor – and here's his name – look. Wow, this *is* a find! He dropped it when he came raiding our cave last night!'

They all crowded round him in excitement. Peter's finger pointed to a name scribbled at the front of the notebook.

'Albert Tanner,' he said. 'He's our mysterious visitor. Albert Tanner! Who can he be? Well, we'll find out *somehow*!'

9 An exciting plan

'Let's clear out of here quickly,' said Colin, in a low voice, looking nervously all round the cave. 'If Albert Tanner, whoever he is, is anywhere near, as he does seem to be, we don't want him to know we've found his notebook. We're all ready to go. Let's scoot off quickly, and examine the notebook in secret.'

'Good idea,' said Peter. 'Ready everyone? Come on then! Scamper, to heel!'

They left the cave and went out into the bright sunshine, each carrying a load. The tins, alas, were now empty, and very light to carry. Half Colin's *Famous Five* books were gone, so he hadn't a great load, either. Most of the magazines had disappeared too. Evidently their mysterious visitor was quite a reader!

They went through the quarry and into Peter's garden. 'We'll go to the summer-house, I think,' said Peter. 'It's not very comfortable, but at least we can talk in secret there.'

Soon they were all sitting on the little bench

that ran round the old summer-house, with Scamper panting on the floor in a patch of warm sunshine.

Peter took the worn notebook out of his pocket and opened it. The others crowded as near as possible to see what was in it. Peter turned over the pages.

'Albert Tanner has written his name in the front as you know,' he said. 'Which was kind of him, I must say – we at least know the *name* of our visitor now! There doesn't seem much else in the book, actually. Just a few notes of money and various dates, and a few words scribbled here and there. Let's see – yes – "potatoes, turnips, tomatoes, flour", just a shopping list, I suppose.'

He turned over a page or two. 'Another shopping list, and some figures jotted down. It doesn't seem as if this notebook is going to be of any use at all!'

Jack took it from him and looked through it too. At the back was a folded-in piece of leather to hold paper money. Peter hadn't noticed it. Jack slipped his fingers in to see if anything could be there.

Yes, a slip of paper, small and torn, with something scribbled on it in a different handwriting from Albert Tanner's.

'Look here!' said Jack. 'This was in the back of the notebook. See what it says? It's a note to Albert Tanner.'

'What does it say?' asked Janet, excited. 'Anything of use to us?'

'It's just scribble,' said Jack, screwing up his eyes. 'It says, "Daren't write it. Jim knows the place. He'll tell you. Meet him on post office seat 8.30 p.m., 15th. Ted."'

'The 15th! That's today,' said Peter. 'Read it again, it's evidently an important message, but how mysterious! What's this "place" Jim is going to tell Albert? My word, if only we could know it! We could go to the "place" Jim says and have a good snoop round.'

A little feeling of excitement began to stir in everyone. Colin caught hold of Peter's sleeve.

'I'll go to the post office seat tonight and sit there. Perhaps I shall see this "Jim" and hear what he says to Albert. I shall *see* Albert too!'

There was a silence, and the excitement suddenly grew stronger. 'A few of us should go,' said Peter. 'Not just you.'

'You can't,' said Janet. 'You're going to see "*Westward Ho!*" at the cinema. Mother's taking us both. And George is coming too, don't you remember?'

'Bother!' said Peter. 'Well, we can't get out of that without giving the whole thing away. Colin, you and Jack must go. And for goodness' sake listen hard and hear what's being said!'

'Right,' said Colin, thrilled. 'Can you come, Jack?'

'Oh yes!' said Jack. 'And what about us shadowing Albert and Jim, Peter? One of us could follow Albert, and the other one could follow Jim. It might be useful to know where Jim lives, and I must say I'd like to follow Albert if he goes back to the cave!'

'A jolly good idea,' said Peter. 'I only wish I could come too. But it's no good. I begged and begged to go to "*Westward Ho!*" and I can't get out of it now.'

They pored over the little note again, written in a bad handwriting, hurried and careless. Peter read it out aloud once more.

'Daren't write it. Jim knows the place. He'll tell you. Meet him on post office seat 8.30 p.m., 15th. Ted.'

'Would there be something hidden in this "place" that is in the note, do you think?' said Janet.

'Yes. Probably,' said Peter, thinking hard. 'And if it's hidden, it's valuable. And if it's valuable it may be stolen goods.'

'Yes. Goods stolen by Ted, whoever he is, and hidden away!' said Colin. 'Or stolen by Ted *and* Albert – and Ted hid them – then got caught, perhaps, and went to prison. And now he wants Albert to find them.'

Everyone laughed. 'You've made quite a story of it!' said Jack. 'I don't expect it's anything like that really. All the same, as soon as we know the place we'll certainly go there – if only we can get there before Albert does!'

'Yes, that's not going to be so easy!' said Peter. 'Maybe Albert will go there at once.'

'I hope he does!' said Colin. 'We'll be shadowing him, and he'll lead us right to this mysterious "place", wherever it is!'

'I wish I was going to be with you tonight,' said Peter longingly. 'It's an adventure, you know, and they don't come very often. I WISH I was going to share it!'

10 What happened at half-past eight

Colin met Jack that evening at eight o'clock outside the post office. It was dark, and there was no moon. They spoke together in low voices as they went over to the wooden seat nearby.

'What shall our plans be?' said Colin. 'The seat is just by that big chestnut tree. Shall we hide behind the tree, or get under the seat, or what?'

'We mustn't both of us be in the same place,' said Jack. 'Otherwise if the men see us and send us off, we'll neither of us hear a word. I vote one of us gets *behind* the tree, and the other *up* the tree!'

'That's a very good idea,' said Colin. 'You'd better climb up the tree. I've got a stiff knee, and it's bandaged. I fell down our cellar steps today, and Mother made a tremendous fuss, and I was afraid she'd make me rest in bed or something! I nearly had a fit, thinking I might not be able to come this evening!'

'All right. I'll climb the tree,' said Jack. 'But I'd better do it now, before anyone comes. There's nobody about at all. I'll stand on the back of the seat, and you can give me a leg-up to that big branch that overhangs the seat.'

It wasn't long before Jack was perched in the thick branches of the chestnut tree. Colin went behind the tree and leaned against the trunk, waiting. The church clock chimed a quarter past eight. Colin's heart began to beat faster – this *was* fun!

Ten minutes went by, and then someone came up. No, two people, arm-in-arm. Colin stiffened and held his breath. The two people passed talking together. Then someone else walked by smartly with a dog.

And then somebody came slouching along in rubber-soled shoes, a shadowy someone who kept out of the light of the street-lamps. He sat down on the seat, and Colin almost stopped breathing!

Jack peered down cautiously from the tree, but it was so dark that he could make out very little except that the man was wearing a cap.

Another shadowy figure appeared from across the road, walking silently. It joined the man on the seat. The two men sat a little apart, saying nothing, and the listening boys held their breath again.

After a few minutes of silence, the first man spoke. 'You're Albert. That's right, isn't it?'

But, before Albert could even nod his head, something happened that made the two men almost jump out of their skins.

Colin sneezed! He always had a very loud sneeze indeed, but this one was tremendous! He didn't even know it was coming, and it gave him almost as much of a shock as it gave the two men!

'A . . . WHOOOOOSH – ooo!'

In a trice Albert had whipped behind the tree and got hold of the startled Colin. He held him in a grip of iron. 'What are you doing here? Hiding behind this tree?'

He shook poor Colin until the boy felt as if his head would fly off. The other man came round the tree too.

'It's only a kid,' he said. 'Let him go. We don't want any noise here.'

Colin got a blow on the head and went staggering away, almost falling. Albert ran at him again, and the boy fled for his life, terrified. Jack, up in the tree, felt very scared too. Should he go to

Colin's rescue? No, by the time he'd got down the tree it would be too late. Ah, Colin had run away, so he was all right. Jack clung to the branch, trembling a little.

The men stood under the tree together. 'Better clear off,' said the first man, in a low voice to Albert.

'You've got something to tell me,' said Albert.

'Yes. The scarecrow!' said his companion, lowering his voice. 'That's where it is. Look by the scarecrow.'

'Thanks,' said Albert, and slouched off silently, and was soon lost in the shadows. Jack wished Colin could have shadowed him. *He* certainly couldn't shadow Albert, because it would take him a minute or two to get cautiously down the tree. Perhaps he could follow the first man, though.

By the time Jack was safely down the tree both men had completely disappeared. Jack made off as quickly as he could, feeling decidedly scared. Was Colin all right? He'd better go to his house and see if he could find out, without letting anyone else know why he had come!

When he arrived at Colin's house he saw a light in Colin's bedroom window. Good! He threw up a pebble and hit the window-pane first time. The window was opened cautiously, and Colin's head came out.

'Colin! It's me, Jack! Are you all right?' called Jack, in a low voice.

'Yes. Quite. That man gave me a jolly good box on the ear, but I got home all right, and no one saw me coming in. What about you? Did you hear anything?'

'Yes, but nothing *really* helpful,' said Jack. 'What a terrific sneeze that was of yours, Colin!'

'Yes, my goodness. I thought I . . .' began Colin, and then drew his head in quickly. Jack heard him speaking to someone in his bedroom, and ran out of the gate as quickly as he could.

The *scarecrow*! he thought. What does that mean? *I* don't know! Perhaps Peter will. Gosh, I can hardly wait until tomorrow morning to tell him!

11   Off they go again!

The meeting in the summer-house the next morning was quite exciting. Peter and Janet and Scamper waited impatiently for Jack and Colin to come. Pam and Barbara came together as usual, then came George, and last of all Colin and Jack.

'Sorry we're a bit late,' said Jack. 'I went to call for Colin. His leg's still stiff so he couldn't walk very fast, though you ran fast enough last night didn't you, Colin?'

Colin grinned. He had a bruise on the left cheekbone near his ear, where he had been struck the night before. He felt rather proud of it.

'We've got news,' said Jack, feeling extremely important as he looked round at the expectant faces of the others.

'Well, hurry up and tell us then,' said Peter impatiently. 'Did those two men meet? What did you hear?'

'Tell it all from the beginning,' begged Janet. 'I like to know every single thing so that I can see it in my mind's eye.'

'All right,' said Jack. 'Well, Colin and I met by the post office at eight o'clock, and the men came at half-past. Colin hid behind a tree, and I climbed up into it.'

'Well done,' said Peter approvingly.

'Just as the men were beginning to talk Colin did the most TERRIFIC sneeze you ever heard,' said Jack. 'Honestly, I nearly fell out of the tree!'

'Gosh!' said Janet. 'Whatever happened then?'

'The men ran round the tree and found poor old Colin, and that bruise on his cheek is where he got hit,' said Jack. Everyone gazed in awe at Colin's bruise, and he felt very proud indeed.

'He had to run for his life, and there was I, stuck up the tree,' went on Jack, enjoying himself immensely. 'I can tell you, it was quite an adventure! Well, then the men spoke in low voices again, but I managed to hear the important thing.'

'What was it?' demanded Peter. 'You're so long-winded. Get to the point.'

'The first man – he must have been the Jim mentioned in the letter – he said "*The scarecrow!*"' said Jack, lowering his voice just as the men had done. '"The scarecrow! That's where it is!" he said. "The scarecrow!" Then the two men went off, and I hadn't time to shadow them because I was up the tree.'

'You did very well,' said Peter. 'Extremely well! It was a pity about Colin's sneeze. Still, you heard the main thing, Jack – and that was the word "scarecrow".'

'What does it mean, though?' asked Jack. 'Do *you* know? Does it mean a *real* scarecrow?'

'No. There's a tiny inn called "The Scarecrow" up on the common,' said Peter. 'I've often passed it when I've been in the car with my father. We'll go up there and snoop round. I bet that's where something is hidden, loot from some robbery, probably.'

'Oh, yes, *I* remember seeing that inn too, and thinking what an odd name it had,' said Janet. 'Peter, let's go *now*! Before Albert gets away with anything!'

'Yes. We'd certainly better go now, this very minute!' said Peter. 'We may find Albert there, digging away in some corner of the garden. It would be very interesting to see what he digs up!'

Everyone felt the delicious surge of excitement that always came over them when adventure was in the air. 'Get your bikes,' ordered Peter. 'Colin, is your knee too stiff to bike, do you think?'

'I can pedal all right with one leg,' said Colin, who wasn't going to be left out of this morning's excitement for anything. 'Come on, let's get our bikes, those of you who didn't come on them.'

'Meet at the crossroads by the old barn,' said Peter. 'Wait for each other. Then we'll all set off together. We're really on to something now!'

George was the only one who had come on a bike. The others set off to get theirs. Peter and Janet fetched their two from the shed, and set off with George to the cross-roads, Scamper running excitedly behind them. He knew when adventure was about, he always knew!

Soon everyone was at the cross-roads, even Colin, who could only pedal with one leg. Jack came last, looking hot and cross.

'What's up?' asked Janet, seeing how upset he looked. 'Did you get into trouble at home about anything?'

'No. It's Susie,' said Jack, with a groan. 'She says that she and Jeff went up to our cave this morning, you know I had to tell Mother about it in front of Susie, and when she saw we'd gone, she and Jeff decided to have it for their meeting-place! Isn't that maddening?'

'Well, let them if they want to!' said Peter. 'Much good may it do them! Albert will probably visit them as he did us and take their things! Serve them right!'

'I wonder how Albert gets into the cave if he doesn't use our entrance!' said Janet. 'We know he used it once, because Jack saw him that time, when we were playing hide-and-seek. But he didn't use it when he robbed us of all those things. Those silk threads at the entrance weren't broken, you remember!'

'I imagine that our dear friend Albert may be somewhere at the inn called "*The Scarecrow*"!' said Peter. 'He probably won't be using the cave much more if he finds what he's looking for!'

'Look, there it is – "*The Scarecrow*"!' said Pam, riding ahead. 'What a funny old inn, hundreds of years old, I should think. Come on, everybody – isn't this EXCITING!'

12   *The Scarecrow Inn*

The Secret Seven came near to the old inn. It was certainly a strange place, almost tumble-down. Outside a sign swung in the wind, creaking dismally. On it was painted a scarecrow in a field, and printed on it in big letters was the name.

'The Scarecrow,' said Peter, leaping off his bicycle. 'Here we are. Look out for Albert, everyone!'

They leaned their bicycles against a hedge and walked over to the inn. No one was about. The whole place looked completely deserted.

'But there must be somebody about!' said Colin. 'Look, there are a few hens pecking around.'

They went right up to the old inn. 'It seems to be shut,' said Peter, puzzled. 'Yes, look, there are bars across the windows and across the front door too, wooden bars, nailed on.'

'It must be closed down,' said Jack. 'Let's go round to the back. We can ask for a drink of water, or how to get to Penton, or something like that.'

So they all went round to the back door of the inn. A woman was in a little yard there, hanging out some washing, an old, grey-haired woman with a very disagreeable face.

'Er, could we have a drink of water, please?' asked Peter, in his politest voice.

'There's the well. Help yourself,' said the woman.

'Thank you. Is the inn closed now?' asked Peter.

'Yes. Been closed for months,' said the old woman, pegging up a sheet. 'I just caretake, and it's a lonely job up here on the common. You're the first people I've spoken to for about six weeks, except for the milkman and the grocer's boy.'

'Oh, then you don't know anyone called Albert, I suppose?' asked Peter, as innocently as he could.

'Now, don't you be cheeky,' said the woman angrily. 'Who told you my old man was called Albert? You call him Mr Larkworthy, and mind your manners. See, there he is. I'll send him after you if you're cheeky!'

The Secret Seven saw an old bent man coming

out of the inn with a stick in his hand, on which he leaned heavily. Goodness, they hadn't meant to be cheeky! How could they have guessed that the old woman's husband was called Albert?

'We didn't mean your husband,' said Peter hurriedly. 'We really didn't. We're just looking for someone called Albert that we thought we might see here this morning.'

'Well, I won't have any cheek from children,' said the old woman. 'You clear off, now, before I tell my husband to chase you.'

The Seven went away slowly, taking a good look at the little place as they went. They walked to their bicycles by the hedge.

'What do you think, Peter,' asked Jack. 'Do you suppose Albert came here at all?'

'No,' said Peter. 'We're on the wrong track. I think that cross old woman was speaking the truth. She probably hasn't seen anyone here for weeks! Gosh, I did feel awful when she said her husband's name was Albert! No wonder she thought we were cheeky!'

'I had a good look at that little garden,' said George. 'And it's quite plain that nobody has been digging in it to get anything buried there. Nothing but enormous weeds.'

'Yes. I had a look too,' said Peter. 'No, we're on

the wrong track, as I said. The thing is, what do we do next? If only we knew where Albert was at this moment, it would be a great help!'

'It might not be,' said Jack, with a grin. 'He might be scaring Jeff and Susie in our cave!'

'I hope he is,' said Peter grimly. 'Just like those two to try to annoy us!'

'What are we going to do now?' asked Janet. 'Peter, do you suppose it's a *real* scarecrow we have to look for?'

Peter considered. 'Yes, it might be. I was so sure that the old inn was the place meant, that I didn't really think about proper scarecrows. But we can't go chasing over the countryside looking for all the scarecrows in the fields!'

'Yes, we can,' said Colin. 'Quite easily. All we've got to do is to separate, and bike all over the place, and whenever we see a scarecrow, get off and see if anyone has been disturbing the ground by it. I *bet* whatever is hidden is well dug-in beside a scarecrow.'

'Yes. It would be such a good place if the thief wanted to get the loot again,' said Peter. 'I mean, if stolen goods were hidden in a field in the ordinary way, they couldn't be marked in case anyone wondered what the mark was for. A stick or a post or something would call attention to the place and make the farmer examine it. But a scarecrow is a *natural* mark and anything hidden beneath it wouldn't be found until the field was reaped!'

'Yes. And the thief meant to get it before that, as we know!' said George. 'Well, shall we go scarecrow-hunting?'

'Yes,' said Peter, getting on his bicycle. 'But look out for farmers. They mightn't be too pleased to see us walking all over their fields to get to a scarecrow!'

They all rode off together, Peter calling out orders as they went.

'You take the west road, Colin and Jack. You the east, Pam and Barbara. You take the north, George, and Janet and I will turn at the cross-roads and take the south. We shall cover most of the countryside then. Meet at half-past two this afternoon in the summer-house.'

Off they all went. 'Scarecrow-hunting!' said Jack to Colin. 'What a game! I do wonder how many scarecrows we shall find!'

The Seven had a strange time, hunting for scarecrows! Pam and Barbara found a most fearsome one in the middle of a field, his coat flapping like mad in the wind.

They went to examine him, but as the soil was

quite hard all round him they knew that nothing had been hidden and dug up beside *him*! So off they went to find another.

Colin and Jack found two. One was in an allotment, and although they were sure that it couldn't be the one they were looking for, they went up to him all the same, and examined the ground nearby.

A man came into the allotment with a spade over his shoulder. When he saw the two boys there he shouted at them angrily:

'You clear off, you two! These allotments are private. Are you the kids who've been talking broccoli from here?'

'No!' shouted the two boys. 'We were just having a look at the old scarecrow.'

'I'll scarecrow you if you come here again!' yelled the man, and Colin and Jack fled for their bicycles. The next scarecrow they found was in a field of young wheat, and no sooner had they walked over the field to the scarecrow than a farmer appeared with a dog. The boys just had time to make sure that the earth round the scarecrow was undisturbed before the dog flew at them.

'Ha! He'll bite you next time!' called the farmer, as the boys leapt on their bicycles.

'I don't think I like this scarecrow-hunting

much,' said Colin, whose stiff leg was hurting him. 'That's twice we've had to run, and I just can't bend my knee properly.'

George, cycling quickly up and down country roads, thought he spied a scarecrow at the end of a field. He jumped off his bicycle and squeezed through the hedge – only to face a surprised and angry farm-labourer, hoeing vigorously.

'Oh – sorry – I thought you were a scarecrow,' said George very foolishly, backing away through the hedge. The farm-labourer, angry at being called a scarecrow, flung a clod of earth at George. It shattered into bits all over him. George spat some out of his mouth.

'Phoo! That was a good shot on his part!' said George, riding away. 'I don't know that I like this scarecrow business much!'

Peter and Janet had examined four scarecrows, for their particular roads ran between big farms, and great fields lay on either side. One scarecrow had thrilled Janet because a thrush had built a nest in the dented crown of the old scarecrow's hat. Peter could hardly get her away from it!

The other three they had found were not interesting, and quite plainly no one had been into the field to disturb the earth near any of the scarecrows.

Peter felt disheartened as he rode home beside Janet. 'All those scarecrows and not one of them any good to us,' he complained. 'I only hope the others have found the right one.'

They got home just in time for their dinner. Their mother looked in horror at their shoes, which were covered in mud from the soil in two very wet fields they had walked over.

'Where *have* you been?' she said. 'And what in the world were you doing to get your shoes so filthy? Take them off at once, and leave them outside.'

'We went to look at scarecrows, Mummy,' said Janet, 'and we found one with a thrush's nest in his hat! That's how we got our shoes so dirty. But we'll clean them ourselves.'

'You should go and see the scarecrow old James has put up in the oat-field,' said her father, who was already at the table. 'He tells me it's got a robin's nest in each pocket!'

'But how did he know?' said Janet in astonishment. 'He's almost blind, poor old man – he can't even see the clouds now, to tell him the weather.'

'Well, he's not too blind to see that somebody had been walking over his precious oat-field,' said her father. 'He followed the footsteps, and they led him right to the scarecrow – and that's how he found the two robins' nest in the pockets!'

Peter pricked up his ears at once. 'Somebody walking over our oat-field to the scarecrow?' he said. 'Who, Dad – and why?'

'Goodness knows,' said his father. 'There are plenty of foolish townspeople who think they can walk all over growing fields! It was one of them, I expect.'

But Peter felt sure it was Albert! He looked at his mother. He really must go and see! 'Er – please could I just go quickly and look at those robins' nests?' he said desperately.

His mother looked at him in amazement. 'What – *now*? Just as dinner's ready? Don't be silly, dear. The nests won't fly away – they'll be there after dinner!'

Peter looked at Janet, who had read his thoughts. 'WHY didn't we think of our own scarecrow!' she blurted out. 'We see it from our bedroom windows each day. We –'

Peter gave her a sharp kick under the table, and she stopped at once. Goodness, she had nearly given the game away!

'Why all this sudden interest in scarecrows?' inquired her mother. 'I hope it soon wears off. I can't allow you to get your shoes like that again.'

Peter and Janet longed for dinner to be over. As soon as they were allowed to go, they shot out into the garden, and slipped on their dirty shoes.

'It was *our* scarecrow we should have looked at!' said Peter. 'I could kick myself! Come on – let's go now and examine the soil round it. We'll take a fork, in case we may find something, though I'm afraid that Albert has got there first. Hurry up!'

13   Everything seems dull now

Peter and Janet ran down the garden and out of the gate at the bottom. Round the potato-field and over a stile they went, and there was the oat-field, its green rows as bright as emerald!

In the middle of it stood the scarecrow put up by old James. He was a fine one, and wore one of James's old hats, cocked over on one side. He wore a ragged red jersey and an old tweed coat with sagging pockets. A robin flew out of one of them as the children went near.

The scarecrow's ragged trousers flapped in the wind against his two wooden legs. His head was a turnip in which old James had scraped eyes and mouth. He seemed to be grinning at them as they came up, and the wind shook him and made him jig to and fro.

But Peter and Janet didn't look at the scarecrow, or even at the robin's nests in the sagging pockets. They looked at the ground around his wooden legs.

And Peter gave a deep groan that really migh

have come from the old scarecrow! 'We *are* too late, Janet. Look, someone's been here. There are footprints all around and about, not only old James's hobnailed ones, but somebody with rubber-soled shoes – Albert's!'

'Yes,' said Janet, her eyes on the ground. 'And the soil has been well dug up. Something was hidden here, beside the old scarecrow. Oh, Peter, WHY didn't we look here first?'

'It wouldn't have been any good,' said Peter gloomily. 'I expect Albert came last night. He wouldn't come digging here in the daytime. He knew which scarecrow was meant, of course. We didn't! And all the time it was our own scarecrow!'

'Just dig round a bit and see if there's anything left,' said Janet.

'There won't be,' said Peter dolefully. 'I expect whatever it was was in a bag, a strong bag too, to resist the damp.' He dug about with his fork, but brought up nothing except a surprised worm. '*Bother!*' he said. 'I was so excited about this scarecrow business. Now we're too late, Albert has got the stuff, whatever it was, and will be off and away.'

'Yes, I suppose he will,' said Janet dismally. 'I wouldn't be surprised if he knew that it was

hidden in this district and that was why he came
and hid in our cave, so as to be on the spot to speak
to that other man, what was his name? Jim? And
to get the stuff easily.'

'I think you're absolutely right, Janet,' said
Peter. 'And if you are, the stolen stuff, or whatever it was, must have *come* from this district too.
I wonder if there have been any robberies
lately.'

They had a look at the two cosy robins'
nests, both of which had tiny feathered nestlings
inside, and then walked back home. It was
about half-past two, and the other members of
the Secret Seven were waiting in the summer-
house.

They were very downcast at Peter's news.
'Well, we were none of us successful in our
scarecrow-hunt this morning,' said Jack, 'and no
wonder, if the loot had been buried by *your*
scarecrow, Peter. What back luck! If only we'd
been able to dig by your scarecrow last night,
perhaps we'd have got the hidden goods before
Albert.'

'What shall we do now?' asked Pam. 'Everything seems dull suddenly, now that we've not
got our cave any more, and the adventure has
faded away.'

'I'm going up to the cave,' said Jack, standing up. 'I think I left my torch there, high up on a ledge. I hope Albert hasn't taken it! It's rather a nice one, and I'd like to get it if it's still there.'

'Right, we'll all come, just for the walk,' said Peter. 'We could take spades and dig in the old quarry, the sand is moist in parts, and you can model quite well with it. Let's do that.'

So they took four spades from the shed and three trowels, and off they went to the quarry. Jack went up to the cave and then stopped short in surprise.

Someone was there! He could hear excited voices. Then he frowned. He knew *one* voice – it was Susie's! Bother her, now she would mess about round them, and make silly remarks. Who was with her? It sounded like Jeff. What cheek to come to the cave! Just like Susie!

He went into the cave, still frowning. Susie and Jeff were right at the back, scrabbling about. Whatever were they doing?

'Susie!' he called sharply. 'What are you doing here?'

Susie turned round and then came quickly over to her brother. 'Jack! I *am* glad you've come. Something peculiar has happened!'

'What?' asked Jack impatiently. 'I think it's pretty peculiar that you and Jeff should come to *our* cave, even though we've left it.'

'Don't be cross, Jack. I really am glad you've come,' said Susie. 'Listen. Jeff and I came here, and we thought it was a lovely place. We made deep holes for ourselves. Mine's over there, look, and Jeff's is opposite, by the rocky wall. We thought perhaps you others might be coming, so we practically *covered* ourselves with sand, just left our noses out to breathe, and we waited for you so that we could give loud yells and leap out at you when you came in thinking nobody was here –'

Jack gave a snort. 'Is that all you've got to tell me? *Not* very interesting.'

'Oh, *do* listen, Jack,' said Susie. 'Well, we lay like mice, only our noses out, waiting for you to come in at the front entrance there, and then somebody came out from the *back* of the cave, and trod heavily on poor Jeff and went out of the entrance!'

'And yet we *know* the cave was empty when we came in,' said Jeff. 'We looked to make sure. But there's nowhere for anyone to hide or to come from, so who was this person, and how did he get here?'

Jack was now listening intently. This was news! He turned to the entrance of the cave and yelled loudly: 'PETER! JANET! EVERYBODY! COME HERE QUICKLY! QUICKLY, I SAY!'

14 What an excitement!

Peter, Janet, and all the others threw down their spades and trowels and raced to the cave at top speed. 'What is it?' cried Peter.

Then he saw Susie and Jeff and stopped. 'Clear out,' he cried. 'This is our cave, not yours.'

'Wait, Peter,' said Jack. 'Susie's just told me something strange.' He told the others what Susie had said, how she and Jeff had buried themselves all but their noses in the empty cave, and then someone had come from the back and walked out!

'So there *is* some way into this cave from the back,' he said. 'I know we've looked and looked, but there *must* be! Susie, did you hear anything at all before this man walked out of the cave?'

'Yes,' said Susie. 'I heard a kind of thud – so did Jeff.'

'As if someone had leapt down to the sandy floor,' said Jeff. 'Like this!' He jumped into the air and came down, making a soft thud.

'Then the way in from the back must be from

somewhere up near the roof,' said Peter. 'Anyone got a torch?'

'Here's mine,' said Jack. 'I found it on the ledge where I'd left it.'

Peter took it. 'Come on,' he said. 'We're jolly well going to solve this mystery. Wait though – Colin, keep guard at the front of the cave, in case that man comes back. Take a good look at him if he does.'

'Right,' said Colin, and limped to the front of the cave, though he would dearly have liked to be with the others.

There was quite a crowd at the back of the cave. Peter shone his torch on to the roof there. It was fairly high. He saw a rocky ledge jutting out and thought he would climb up to it. 'Give me a hand,' he said to Jack. 'Hold the torch for a minute, Janet.'

He was soon up on the ledge, and then shone the torch on to the roof again. He gave a sudden exclamation.

'What is it?' shouted everyone, almost dancing with excitement.

'There's a round hole here. You can't see it from where you are,' said Peter. 'And there's a rope-end hanging down. I can just reach it.'

The others craned their necks to see what Peter

saw, but they couldn't. The hole was hidden by a jutting-out piece of rock, and it was only because Peter was high up on the ledge that he could see it at all. He shone his torch on the thick rope-end. It was well within his reach from the ledge on which he stood.

He stuffed the torch into his pocket. 'I can get hold of the rope,' he called down, 'and I think I can pull myself up by it. I'll try anyway.'

He caught the rope in both hands, and then by means of treading on first one narrow ledge of rock and then another, he managed to get right into the hole. He let go of the ledges with his feet and swung on the rope with his hands. He climbed up it as he did at gym, and came to a broad ledge, where he rested for a moment or two.

Then he stood on the ledge, putting his head up through the hole that still went upwards, and found that he was looking out of the hole into another cave above! He shone his torch around.

He gave a yell to the others down below, but to them his voice sounded curiously muffled and hollow. They were quite startled to hear it.

'Hey! There's another cave here, a much smaller one! And some of our food's here, and all our cushions, and books and magazines! And there's a bag too, a small mail-bag that looks full of something!'

'What? What do you say?' yelled the others, almost overcome with excitement at all this shouting, and not being able to make out a word.

'PETER! What have you found?' cried Janet.

Peter came down from the rope, found the ledge he needed to climb down from, and leapt to the ground. He pushed the others away as they crowded round him, and went to get some air at the front of the cave.

'Tell us! What did you find?' said Jack. 'We heard you yelling.'

'There's a cave up there with all our things in it. That man Albert used the cushions to lie on, because the floor is of hard rock, not soft sand,' said Peter. '*And* there's a bag, a mail-bag, I think. Probably full of registered envelopes! Goodness knows how long it was buried beneath our scarecrow.'

'Well, that's a find!' said Janet, her eyes shining. 'Now we know how our mysterious visitor got into the cave without passing through the front entrance, when he wanted to steal our things. How thrilled he must have been to find food and cushions and books!'

'Now listen,' said Peter. 'He may come back at any minute, he won't dare to come into the cave while people are there. I'm going to tell Dad, and he'll phone the police. You stay here, all of you, till I come back, then Albert won't be able to remove the stolen mailbag! I'll leave Scamper with you too.'

'Right,' said Jack, taking charge. 'We'll make a good bit of noise too, shall we, to scare him off if he comes! Well done finding that cave above, Peter. You *are* clever!'

'Well, *I* really put you on to it,' said Susie. 'Gosh, I was glad to see you, Jack.'

'You were wrong to come to our cave, but for once in a way you were right to tell me what you'd seen,' said Jack sternly. 'Now, if you want to stay with us, behave yourself, Susie. Do you hear?'

'Yes, teacher,' said Susie demurely. 'I'll be a good, good girl. I'll –'

'Be quiet,' said Jack, 'or out you both go, you and Jeff!'

Susie looked at Jack's face and was suddenly quiet. They all were for a minute or two, thinking over the startling happenings of the last few minutes. Then they remembered that Peter wanted them to make a noise, so that Albert would not come to the cave to try to get that mailbag! They began to talk and laugh.

Peter ran at top speed to find his father. 'Dad!' he called, seeing him by the barn. 'Hey, DAD! Quick, I want you!'

15   A wonderful finish!

Peter's father could not make head or tail of the boy's breathless story at first. But at last he made out enough to call his wife.

'Will you telephone to the police and tell them to come at once, and go to the cave in the quarry?' he called. 'I'm off there with Peter. Tell you what's up when I get back!'

He went off with the excited Peter. Soon they were at the cave, where the others, talking loudly, were waiting anxiously. The green curtain was tied back now, and Peter's father gazed into the cave.

'I'd forgotten this old cave,' he said. 'I used to love it when I was a boy. Do you really mean to say there's a cave *above* it, Peter? I never knew that, and yet I played here heaps of times.'

'So did we,' said Janet. 'Come and see where the hole is that leads into the cave above, Daddy.'

'We had this cave for our Secret Seven meetings,' explained Peter, 'and we *couldn't* make out who took our things, or why. We didn't guess someone was in hiding in a cave above us! There's a mail-bag up there, Dad. Do you think the man stole it?'

'Probably. You'd better shin up and get it when the police come,' said Peter's father. 'I wonder how long it's been hidden there? Quite a long time, maybe.'

'No, only since last night,' said Peter. 'It was buried beside that scarecrow in the oat-field, Dad!'

'So *that's* why you were so interested in scarecrows all of a sudden,' said his father. 'I wonder if your mother has telephoned the police yet. Run back and see if they're coming, Peter.'

Peter set off through the quarry with Scamper at his heels, but halfway through Scamper left him and ran behind a hummock, barking madly. Peter followed him. He saw a curious mound in the sand, which, as Scamper leapt on it, put out hands and feet – and head!

'Call him off!' said a voice. 'Call him off!'

'Who are you?' demanded Peter, catching Scamper by the collar. 'Hey, *I* know who you are, you're Albert, aren't you? Waiting till we're all gone so that you can fetch that stolen mail-bag and empty it! You meant to leave the bag up in that cave, stuff your pockets with the contents, and slip away free! You'll –'

'Now, now,' said a deep voice, 'what's all this, and who is this fellow lying in the sand? Ah, surely it's Albert Tanner! We've been looking for you, Albert, ever since that last mail robbery.'

It was the big Inspector of Police! Behind him was a stolid village constable, looking as if this kind of thing was very ordinary indeed.

The Inspector turned to Peter and beamed at him. 'Hello, Peter! I knew as soon as your mother phoned that you were caught up into one of your adventures. Is Albert here anything to do with it?'

'Yes,' said Peter. 'Look, my father's over there, by the cave. He's waiting for you.'

'Bring Albert along,' said the Inspector to his policeman, and Albert was duly brought along to the cave. As soon as Peter's father saw him, he gave an exclamation.

'Why! It's Albert Tanner! I thought I told you never to show your face in this district again, Albert!'

'You know him, sir, do you?' said the Inspector, getting out a big note-book.

'I should think I do!' said Peter's father. 'He was brought up here on this land, in a cottage not far

off, and worked for me for a few years. But he
was so dishonest I had to dismiss him.'

'That's how he knew this cave then!' said Peter.
'*And* the one above. He must have explored like
we did.'

Albert didn't say a word. He stood there, sullen
and angry. The Inspector threw a glance at him.
Then he turned to Peter's father.

'This man and another did a mail-bag robbery,'
he said. 'The other man hid the bag somewhere,
meaning to get it when the commotion about it
died down. He worked on this farm once too, sir –
his name's Ted Yorks.'

'Ted Yorks! Yes, he was here for years,' said
Peter's father. 'He was a bad lot too, but a fine
hedger and ditcher, which is why I kept him so
long.'

'Well, as I said, these two planned this robbery,'
said the Inspector, 'and the mail-bag was hidden,
ready to be found and the contents shared between the two of them in due course. But Ted got
caught and put into prison, where he is still.'

'But he managed to get a note out of prison to
Albert, to tell him how to find out where he had
hidden the bag!' cried Peter. 'I see it all now!
Albert came to this cave to hide till he heard from
Ted, because he knew the police here were still

looking for him, and he didn't dare to show his face –'

'And when he got Ted's note, he went to meet that man Jim, the one on the seat by the post-office, and learnt that he had to look by the scarecrow!' said Jack. 'I heard Jim say "The Scarecrow. That's where it is." And of course, Albert knew it was *our* scarecrow!'

'These kids know all about you, you see, Albert,' said the Inspector, looking at the surly man. 'Where did you put that mail-bag after you'd dug it up, Albert?'

'I'm not saying anything,' said Albert, 'except that I don't know anything about any mail-bag, and it's no use asking me.'

'I'll get the mail-bag, shall I?' said Peter, much to the Inspector's surprise. He looked at Peter, quite astounded.

'The mail-bag? Don't tell me you know where *that* is?' he said. 'Right, get it.'

So off went Peter to the back of the cave, shinned up the wall, caught hold of the rope, and disappeared. Then a voice came down the hole.

'Stand by, everyone! Mail-bag on the way!' There was a heavy thud on the soft sand, and there was the mail-bag! Its fall had broken it open, and registered envelopes and packets came tumbling out.

'Whew!' said the Inspector, amazed. 'This is magic! Hey, Peter, any more mail-bags to come?'

Peter came down the hole, laughing. 'No. That's the only one. Is it the stolen one?'

'Yes,' said the Inspector. 'Well, I'm afraid Albert won't be able to steal any more mail-bags for a long, long time. Take him away, Constable!'

Albert was marched away, still sullen and silent. 'Come in and have a word with my wife, Inspector,' said Peter's father. 'She must be longing to know what all this excitement's about. Peter, here's some money. Take all the Secret Seven out and give them a thumping good tea, ice-creams and all. You've done well, my boy!'

He went off with the Inspector, who waved a cheery hand to them. Peter turned to the others, beaming. He waved the money at them.

'Look at that! We'll have a feast. Come on!'

Susie and Jeff went out of the cave with the others. Jack gave his sister a little push.

'You're not coming with *us*, Susie. We're the Secret Seven, and you don't belong. You go home.'

'Oh,' said Janet, seeing Susie's downcast face, 'couldn't she come just for once? I mean, she did tell you about Albert coming out of the back of the cave when she and Jeff were there, Jack, and it was because of that that we managed to find the other cave at last. *Couldn't* she come?'

'No. We're the Secret Seven,' said Jack, 'and Susie would only laugh and sneer at us all the time, like she always does. And Jeff too. No.'

'I won't! I think you're wonderful!' said Susie. 'Let me come. Just this once, Jack. I DO want to hear all about this exciting adventure.'

'You can come, Susie,' said Peter, taking command. '*And* Jeff too. Just this once. It's a story worth telling, I promise you. It will take us at least four ice-creams each before the tale is told. It's a jolly good adventure, you'll have to admit that, Susie!'

It was, and Susie's going to say so, too, when she's heard it. Good old Secret Seven – they always get there in the end, don't they?

THE ENID BLYTON NEWSLETTER

Would you like to receive The Enid Blyton Newsletter? It has lots of news about Enid Blyton books, videos, plays, etc. There are also puzzles and a page for your letters. It is published three times a year and is free for children who live in the United Kingdom and Ireland.

If you would like to receive it for a year, please write to: The Enid Blyton Newsletter, PO Box 357, London WC2E 9HQ, sending your name and address. (UK and Ireland only)

A complete list of the SECRET SEVEN ADVENTURES *by Enid Blyton*

A complete list of the FAMOUS FIVE
ADVENTURES *by Enid Blyton*

A Little Princess

Frances Hodgson Burnett

Sara Crewe is the seven year old daughter of a rich and loving father, and has recently come to London from India. At her new school she is nicknamed the Little Princess by her classmates. She has all the comforts and fine things a young girl could want, but she also reveals a kind and loving heart, a lively mind and a rich imagination.

Then her father dies, bankrupt. Sara is suddenly reduced to a life of poverty – she is forced to live in a cold, damp attic, with only her dreams to support her.

But will they be enough?

HODDER CLASSICS

All Hodder Children's books are available at your local bookshop or newsagent, or can be ordered direct from the publisher. Just tick the titles you want and fill in the form below. Prices and availability subject to change without notice.

Hodder Children's Books, Cash Sales Department, Bookpoint, 39 Milton Park, Abingdon, OXON, OX14 4TD, UK. If you have a credit card you may order by telephone – 01235 831700.

Please enclose a cheque or postal order made payable to Bookpoint Ltd to the value of the cover price and allow the following for postage and packing: UK & BFPO: £1.00 for the first book, 50p for the second book, and 30p for each additional book ordered up to a maximum charge of £3.00.
OVERSEAS & EIRE: £2.00 for the first book, £1.00 for the second book, and 50p for each additional book.

Name ....

Address ....

....

....

If you would prefer to pay by credit card, please complete:
Please debit my Visa/Access/Diner's Card/American Express (delete as applicable) card no:.

Signature ....

Expiry Date ....